Reduce, Reuse, Recycle

Helen Lanz

SEA-TO-SEA
Mankato Collingwood London

This edition first published in 2012 by

Sea-to-Sea Publications
Distributed by Black Rabbit Books
P.O. Box 3263, Mankato, Minnesota 56002

Copyright © Sea-to-Sea Publications 2012

Printed in China

9 8 7 6 5 4 3 2

Published by arrangement with the Watts
Publishing Group Ltd, London.

Library of Congress Cataloging-in-Publication Data

Lanz, Helen.
  Reduce, reuse, recycle / by Helen Lanz.
     p. cm. -- (Go green)
  Includes index.
  ISBN 978-1-59771-303-0 (library binding)
  1. Waste minimization--Juvenile literature. 2. Recycling (Waste,
etc.)--Juvenile literature. I. Title.
  TD793.9.L36 2012
  363.72'82--dc22
                                        2011004378

Series Editor: Julia Bird
Design: D.R. ink
Artworks: Mike Phillips

Picture credits: Monica Adamczyk/istockphoto: 16b;
Arvind Balarman/Shutterstock: 12bl; Blackbeck/istockphoto: 27b;
Jeffrey Blacker/Alamy: 23b; Bubbles/Alamy: 20t; Tony Campbell/
istockphoto: 11b; Cultura/Getty Images: 1, 26; Randy
Faris/Flame/Corbis: 17; Nick Free/istockphoto: 27t; Ben
Frederick/PD: 20b; Grandpa/Shutterstock: 12tr; David J
Green/Alamy: 15b; Home Studio/Shutterstock: 21t; Stephanie
Horrocks/istockphoto: 13tr: Jupiter Images/Alamy: front cover t;
LACSD: 8; Scott Latham/Shutterstock: 11t; Magnus/Alamy: 16t;
Ian Miles/Flashpoint Pictures/Alamy: 7; David Noble
Photography/Alamy: front cover cr; Paul O'Connor/Alamy: 18bl;
Skip O'Donnell/istockphoto: 24b; Brandon Parry/Shutterstock:
19b; Patrimonio Designs/Shutterstock: 25t; Photoalto/Alamy:
24t; Recycle Now Partners: 19t; Reportage/Getty Images: 10;
Reuters/Corbis: 9; Christina Richards/Shutterstock: 15t;
Hughette Roe/istockphoto: 22b; Ilan Rosen/PD: 21b.
Mark Ross/Shutterstock: 18tr; Vladimir Sazonov/Shutterstock.

To my dad, whose jokes are largely recycled and
all a load of garbage!

February 2011
RD/6000006415/001

"During 25 years of writing about the environment for the Guardian, I quickly realized that education was the first step to protecting the planet on which we all depend for survival. While the warning signs are everywhere that the Earth is heating up and the climate changing, many of us have been too preoccupied with living our lives to notice what is going on in our wider environment. It seems to me that it is children who need to know what is happening—they are often more observant of what is going on around them. We need to help them to grow up respecting and preserving the natural world on which their future depends. By teaching them about the importance of water, energy, and other key areas of life, we can be sure they will soon be influencing their parents' lifestyles, too. This is a series of books every child should read."

Paul Brown
Former environment correspondent
for the UK's *Guardian* newspaper,
environmental author and fellow of
Wolfson College, Cambridge, UK.

Contents

Words in **bold** can be found in the glossary on page 28.

What a Waste!

What have you eaten or used today? Did you have to throw anything away? We all throw things away every day. A wrapper around something we've eaten, an apple core, a piece of paper that we've drawn on. This is our "waste" or garbage.

A Load of Garbage!

Imagine this: if you live in the UK, the United States, or Australia, you probably throw away seven times your weight in garbage every year! This garbage is likely to include three plastic bottles, four glass bottles, 13 metal cans, and 11 pounds (5 kg) of paper a week. The U.S. tops the charts for the country that makes the most waste, Australia comes second, and the UK throws away the most garbage of any country in Europe.

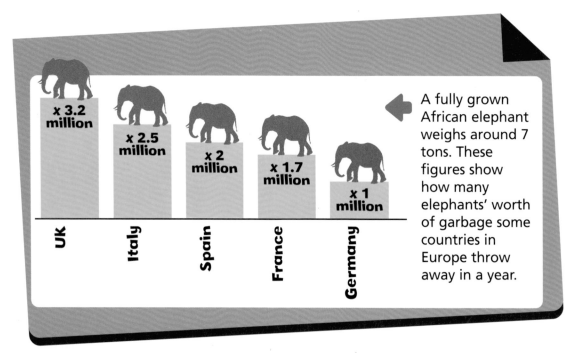

x 3.2 million — UK
x 2.5 million — Italy
x 2 million — Spain
x 1.7 million — France
x 1 million — Germany

A fully grown African elephant weighs around 7 tons. These figures show how many elephants' worth of garbage some countries in Europe throw away in a year.

In Europe, about 3,500 trash cans full of garbage are thrown away every minute. ➡

Why So Much Garbage?

We haven't always made so much waste. Nowadays, food and other goods are much more heavily packaged than they used to be, meaning we have more **packaging** to throw away. We also tend to buy more products, such as clothes, toys, and electrical goods, than people used to, and we keep them for less time before throwing them away. Most importantly, there are many more of us in the world than there used to be. The Earth's **population** has multiplied by four times in the last 100 years, and more people equals more waste.

What Happens to Our Waste?

There are lots of ways of disposing of waste, but to get rid of most of our garbage, we dig huge holes in the ground and bury it. This is known as **landfill**. We can also burn or **recycle** garbage.

The Puente Hills Landfill is currently the biggest landfill in the U.S. It receives 13,000 tons of garbage every day.

Burying the Problem

In landfill sites, the waste is placed in holes, or "cells," which are lined with plastic to stop the waste from **polluting** the soil. However, as the garbage slowly **rots**, liquid waste and gas often leak out. Rotting food makes a gas called **methane**, which leaks into our air, while liquid waste can get into the **groundwater** and pollute our water supplies.Our garbage takes a long time to rot. For example, a plastic bottle can take more than 450 years to break down. This means buried garbage is going to be a problem for a long time to come.

WHAT A DUMP!

While developed countries, such as the United States and UK, bury their garbage, developing countries, such as India, often heap theirs up into massive, rotting piles. This is dangerous and extremely bad for people's health. And what's also shocking is that sometimes this garbage is not from the people themselves, but from people in developed countries who have paid to dump their waste somewhere else.

In Mumbai, India, nearly 500,000 people live near a garbage dump.

Going Up in Smoke

Waste can also be incinerated, or burned. Some countries in Europe, such as Denmark, incinerate more than half their waste. The process gives off several gases, including **carbon dioxide** (CO_2), which are harmful to our environment, though many modern incinerators can use the heat from the incinerator to make electricity.

Recycling

Recycling rates vary around the world, but account for around 32 percent of waste disposal in the U.S. and UK. Garbage is taken to a recycling plant where it is broken down so the **material** it is made from, such as glass, paper, or metal, can be used to make new products, such as bottles, newspapers, and cans.

Did you know?

Up to 80 percent (that's most) of what we throw away could be reused or recycled.

Resources

By simply throwing things away and buying new things, we use up more and more of the Earth's **natural resources**, such as wood, water, and metal. This is because the more products we make, the more resources we use to make them. We also use the Earth's **fossil fuels** to give us the power to actually make the new products.

To make just one computer and its screen uses metal, glass, **chemicals,** 530 lb. (240 kg) of fossil fuels, and 1.5 tons of water.

Fossil Fuels

Coal, oil, and natural gas are known as fossil fuels because they are formed under the ground over millions of years from the remains of plants and animals. Fossil fuels are used to generate electricity, which is used in factories to make new products for us to use and buy. But our supplies of fossil fuels are running out and they cannot be replaced.

Getting Hotter

The Earth is surrounded by a layer of gases called the **atmosphere**. The Sun's rays can shine through this layer, but it also keeps in the Sun's heat. When we burn fossil fuels, they release carbon dioxide. This gas is good at trapping heat so, with more of it in the atmosphere, the Earth is heating up. This is known as **global warming**. As we burn more and more fossil fuels to make products, the rate of global warming is increasing.

 Carbon dioxide traps heat like the glass in a greenhouse. That's why it is also called a **greenhouse gas**.

Climate Change

As the temperature of the Earth changes, it is changing our weather patterns. Extreme weather events around the world, such as floods, **drought**, and violent storms, are becoming more common. This is called **climate change**.

The Earth's climate varies naturally, but floods like this are becoming more common.

SPEED LIMIT 20

Reduce Your Use

Luckily, there is plenty we can all do to help solve our garbage problem. Have you heard of the "three Rs"—reducing, reusing, and recycling? Many of you probably already recycle some of your garbage. But what about "reducing" or "reusing" it?

Cut Down

Reducing is the first step to take in cutting down on waste. Reducing means exactly that—reducing how much waste we make in the first place.

The more we buy, the more waste we produce.

Our Earth is amazing, so let's use its resources carefully.

ONE EARTH OR TWO?

If all of the people on the Earth bought as much as people in the U.S., we would need three to five more new Earths just to fit in all the things that have been bought, and to have enough resources to make all these things in the first place.

Think About It

Reducing our use is all about asking ourselves whether we really need to buy something new, or whether we can get by without it. Companies want us to buy all the latest clothes, toys, and electronic gadgets so they make money, but the truth is that we often lose interest in our new things quite quickly.

It is more likely for us to remember happy events from our childhood rather than the things we had.

Less is Best

When you do decide to buy something, try to choose a product that has less packaging. Some packaging is needed to protect the product, but lots of flashy packaging just creates more waste. Food and drinks packaging helps keep them fresh, but try not to buy individually wrapped items. These have lots of wasteful packaging and are more expensive than buying food and drinks in bulk.

At Christmas in the UK, for example, 800,000 tons of toy packaging—about the same weight as 115,000 African elephants—ends up in landfill.

Can't Reduce? Reuse!

If you've just got to have a new toy, gadget, or game, how about buying one that has already been used, or simply borrowing one for a while? This saves resources and money.

Reusing in Action

We already reuse things, probably without thinking about it. Do you ever borrow books, CDs, or DVDs from the library? Or play with your older brother's or sister's toys? You may even wear "hand-me-downs" from older brothers or sisters. These are all examples of reusing things.

Oh, no. It's not way too big, honey, it just means it'll last you a bit longer!

Pass It On

If you don't want something anymore, don't just throw it out. Give it to a friend or take it to a rummage sale. Or, you can donate old toys, books, and clothes to Goodwill Stores. The sales of your donations support programs that help people in your community and donating to charity can help lower your family's tax bill.

Get Online

It's now really easy to pass on or sell things online. A web site called Freecycle.org can put you in touch with people in your local area who want to find or get rid of all kinds of things, from furniture to bicycles. If you'd like to sell your things instead, you could ask your parents or carer to help you look at web sites such as Ebay.

Goodwill Stores sell secondhand clothes, books, games, and toys to raise money to help people in need.

Selling your old things over the Internet can help to raise money to buy something else (second-hand, of course!).

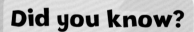

Did you know?

The fossil fuels used to produce one computer chip weigh 600 times the weight of the chip.

Reuse Again

If you want to make the best use of your things, you should also look at what you buy in the first place. Things that are well made will last and can be used again. However, if something does break, instead of throwing it away, perhaps it could be fixed?

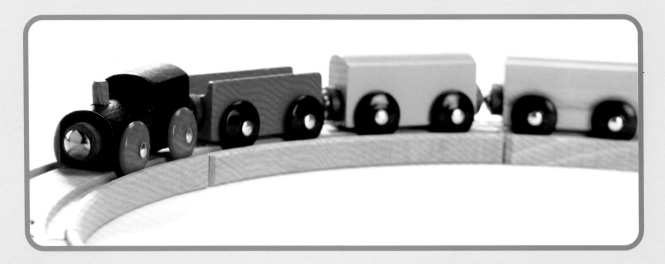

 Toys that are made well last a long time and can be passed on to brothers and sisters, and even the next generation.

Make It Last!

Try to avoid using **disposable** things whenever you can. If you take your lunch to school, try to avoid prepacked snacks that create lots of garbage. If you use plastic plates or cutlery, wash and reuse them. If you're going on vacation, try not to take a disposable camera that you can only use once.

Reuse Your Bags

Take large, sturdy reusable plastic bags with you to use when you go shopping. Plastic bags are bad for the environment because they take so long to break down, or biodegrade, in landfill (see page 8). You can make a difference by reusing your old bags instead of using new ones only once and then throwing them away. Always take reusable bags with you when you shop.

Reusable cloth or hemp bags are stronger than plastic bags, as well as being a lot better for the environment.

PLASTIC IS NOT SO FANTASTIC!

It is believed that in Australia, about 429,000 plastic bags end up in landfill every hour, or 7,150 bags every minute.

In the United States, out of every $10 spent buying things, $1 goes for packaging, which is simply thrown in the garbage. Packaging represents about 65 percent of household trash.

Recycle! Recycle!

If you can't reuse something and it can't be repaired, perhaps the materials that it is made from could be used again? This is recycling. It saves landfill space, **energy**, money, and resources, and helps reduce pollution.

Waste Paper

A lot of the trash in our garbage cans is paper or cardboard waste. We use paper every day in a variety of products, from packaging to phone directories. In the United States, to produce each week's Sunday newspapers, 500,000 trees must be cut down. Companies worldwide use enough paper in a day to wrap around the Earth 20 times.

 Look for the mobius loop on goods and packaging. It shows that something can be recycled.

Wonderful Wood

Wood is a **renewable** resource— trees can be planted and grown specially to be cut down and used to make paper. So, recycling used paper and cardboard saves trees, but also landfill space, energy, and money.

The trees in this forest are specially grown to be made into paper.

How It Works

It is usually easy to recycle paper and cardboard. Most cities have a curbside service where they will pick up waste paper that's been collected at home and take it to a recycling facility. If your city doesn't run a curbside collection, you can take old paper and cardboard to recycling centers in your local area.

New Products

All sorts of products can be made out of recycled paper and cardboard. Newspapers and magazines are mostly made from recycled paper, and you can buy recycled paper writing pads and toilet paper. But recycled paper can also be used to make a variety of other products including building insulation, animal bedding, lampshades, and even ornaments!

Many schools—like this one in the UK—recycle their waste paper.

This colorful pot is made from recycled magazines.

Did you know?

If we recycled all our waste paper, more than 250 million trees could be saved a year.

Glass and Plastic

Did you know that people have dug up glass that is more than 3,000 years old? That tells us that glass doesn't break down very quickly! But it can be recycled over and over again without losing its quality. So don't throw that bottle away—recycle it!

Dos and Don'ts

There are some dos and don'ts about recycling glass. Make sure you wash any bottles or jars out, and separate them by color at home or at the recycling center. Don't put in any heat-resistant glass, such as Pyrex, lightbulbs, or non-see-through glass—these can spoil a whole batch of glass.

 Separate your glass into green, brown, or clear glass before taking it to the recycling center.

New Glass

Once it's been recycled, glass has many uses. It can be remade into bottles or jars, made into jewelry or ornaments, or mixed with other materials and used for building. It is also used to make a substance called glassphalt, and used in road surfaces.

 Glassphalt helps car tires grip the surface of the road.

Plastic Problem

It is thought that some plastic objects could take more than 450 years to break down. So it's scary to think that in the U.S., every hour, more than two million plastic bottles are thrown away and not recycled.

Plastic Dos and Don'ts

Plastic objects can often be recycled along with your household waste, but check first. There are lots of different types of plastic, so make sure the label shows the recycling loop before you put it in the recycling container. Also remember to "wash and squash" before you recycle!

New Plastic

Recycled plastic can be turned into new bottles, yard furniture, carpets, and even clothes. It takes just 25 plastic bottles to make a fleece jacket!

Recycled plastic can be made into colorful raincoats.

Recycling Metal

Did you know that your car could be made out of the same material as a food or beverage can? Aluminum and steel are metals and are used to make all sorts of things, from car parts to packaging. Both metals can be recycled over and over again to make anything from bikes to bridges.

Haven't I seen you somewhere before?

Nearly 60 percent of aluminum used today has been recycled. So your car may well have a few old beverage cans in it!

Save Energy

It takes a lot of energy to make things from fresh aluminum or steel but it *saves* a lot of energy to make things from recycled aluminum and steel. For example, it takes the same amount of energy to make 20 recycled aluminum cans as it does to make one brand new can. Yet at the moment, we only recycle a fraction of the metal that we could.

IN THE CAN

Americans use more than 80,000,000,000 aluminum soda cans a year. Recycling just one aluminum beverage can saves the equivalent of half a gallon (nearly 2 l) of gasoline.

Aluminum cans are crushed before recycling.

THE WAR EFFORT

During World War Two (1939–1945), materials were in short supply because everything was being used in the war effort. Everybody recycled everything they could. In the UK, metal straps were taken from corsets (underwear) and enough metal was saved to build two warships!

Dos and Don'ts

There's plenty you can do to help. Be sure to wash out any cans before recycling. Check foil wrapping to see if it is aluminum; if it springs back to shape, it is not aluminum and cannot be recycled. How about collecting cans at school for "Cans for Cash" centers or "Cans and bottles for a cause" schemes to raise money for your school or charity?

An aluminum beverage can can be recycled, made into a new can, filled, and be back on the shelf in just sixty days.

Recycling Electronics

Many homes in developed countries are full of electronic equipment—from Playstations™ to washing machines. But what do we do with the old products when they break down or newer versions are in the stores? Most are just thrown away.

 More than three-quarters of old electrical appliances end up in landfill.

Friends might enjoy playing with your old computer games.

Think About It

Before you decide to throw away your electronic game, first see whether you can give it to a friend, donate it to a Goodwill Store, or sell it online (see page 15). If it's broken, find out whether it can be repaired.

Use Caution

If your electronic product can't be given away or repaired, check with your local authority to see whether they will pick it up and arrange for it to be recycled, because many cities offer this service. Many electronic items contain dangerous substances that would pollute the environment, so make sure that they are recycled with care.

Symbols such as these indicate that a product shouldn't go in the household trash can. Most electronic goods can't go in the trash can, but many can be recycled.

CASE STUDY
IT'S THE CELL!

Cell phones are built to last for about seven years, but we tend to buy new phones every 11 months or so. About 150 million cell phones a year are thrown away in the U.S.—wasting enough energy to power 285,000 homes for a year. Rather than just throwing your old cell away, try giving it away or recycling it.

Precious metals, such as gold and copper, are found in cell phones and can be reused.

Keep the Loop Going

There are many good reasons to reduce, reuse, and recycle. It can save resources, energy, landfill space, and money, as well as reduce pollution.

Could Do Better!

The good news is that most countries are recycling more each year, but countries such as the U.S. could still recycle about one-third more.

By 2010, Europe has been set the target of recycling at least 60 percent, more than half, of all household waste. The UK government has decided that by this time, at least 74 percent (that's nearly three-quarters) of waste from homes should be recycled and not just thrown away.

 By working together, we can all help to recycle more and more of our garbage.

Power of the People

That's all of us! If we all reduce our use, reuse, and recycle, we can save enormous amounts of natural resources, energy, money, space, and pollution. We all need to look at our habits—do we really need to keep buying more things? If we do need to buy, shop for products made from recycled materials, and once you've finished with these, recycle them again. This truly completes the recycling loop.

Help complete the loop. Recycle your waste, then buy it back as something else!

THE POWER OF RRR

Recycling just under a ton of paper saves 17 trees, 2 barrels of oil, enough energy to power the average home for 6 months, saves enough landfill space to fit a family-size people carrier, and saves more than 60 pounds (27 kg) of air pollution.

Our world is full of beautiful places. It is up to us to protect these places so we can continue to enjoy them in the future.

Glossary

Atmosphere The layer of air around the Earth.

Carbon dioxide A gas in the air around us.

Chemical Something that has been made through a chemical process. For example, detergents are chemicals that clean things by removing dirt particles.

Climate change Long-term changes to the Earth's weather patterns.

Developed countries Countries with highly developed economies, where most of the population work in factories and businesses.

Developing countries Countries with less developed economies, where most of the population work in farming.

Disposable Designed to be thrown away after it has been used.

Drought A shortage of rain over a long period of time.

Energy The power to make or do something.

Fossil fuels Fuels, such as coal, oil, or gas, that have developed under the ground from rotting animal and plant life over millions of years.

Global warming The gradual heating up of the Earth's atmosphere.

Greenhouse gas A gas, such as carbon dioxide, that creates an invisible layer around the Earth, keeping in the heat of the Sun's rays.

Groundwater Water from rain that collects and flows under the Earth's surface.

Landfill Areas for dumping and burying household or industrial waste.

Materials What something is made from, such as cotton, wood, or metal, for example.

Methane A gas produced when food or plants rot. It is also made by animals when they digest (break down) their food. Methane is a powerful greenhouse gas.

Natural resources Materials, such as water and wood, that are found in nature.

Packaging The box or wrapping that surrounds a product.

Polluting Making something, such as water or the air, dirty.

Population The number of people living in a place.

Recycle To break something down so that the materials that it is made from can be used again.

Renewable Something that is in constant supply and will not run out, such as the wind.

Rots When something, such as food, goes moldy and starts to smell bad.

Useful Information

Throughout this book, "real-life measurements" are used for reference. These measurements are not exact, but give a sense of just how much an amount is, or what it looks like.

African elephant = 7 tons

Earth's circumference at equator = 29,200 miles (40,000 km)

Average distance from Earth to the moon= 239,000 miles (384,500 km)

Further Reading

Your Environment: Recycling by Jen Green (Franklin Watts, 2007)

Re-Using and Recycling series by Ruth Thomson (Franklin Watts, 2008)

Let's Find Out About: Recycling by Dr. Mike Goldsmith (ticktock Media Ltd., 2009)

Web Sites

www.olliesworld.com
Tips on how we can all reduce, reuse, recycle, and rethink.

www.resourcefulschools.org/students.html
Fun recycling activities.

www.kidsrecyclingzone.com
All about recycling at home and at school.

Dates to Remember

Earth Hour—28 March 28

Earth Day—22 April 22

World Environment Day—5 June 5

Clean Air Day—June

International Walk to School Campaign—May and October

World Food Day—October 16

America Recycles Day—November 15

Note to parents and teachers: Every effort has been made by the Publishers to ensure that these web sites are suitable for children, that they are of the highest educational value, and that they contain no inappropriate or offensive material. However, because of the nature of the Internet, it is impossible to guarantee that the contents of these sites will not be altered. We strongly advise that Internet access is supervised by a responsible adult.

Index